Thomas Alva Edison was born on February 11, 1847, in Milan, Ohio. His parents were Samuel and Nancy Edison.

Samuel Edison owned a mill which made wood shingles. Nancy Edison had been a teacher. Thomas was the youngest of their seven children.

Thomas was curious and asked his parents many questions. If they didn't know an answer, he asked, "Why don't you know?"

Thomas loved to experiment. He made a nest and filled it with goose and chicken eggs. He sat on the eggs to see if they would hatch. Of course they didn't. The eggs broke and ruined the seat of his pants.

A Picture Book of
Thomas Alva Edison

David A. Adler

illustrated by John & Alexandra Wallner

Holiday House/New York

Other books in David A. Adler's *Picture Book Biography* series

In loving memory of my inventive and heroic brother, Edward M. Adler,
recipient of The Carnegie Hero's Award, 1948–1979

D.A.A.

For Jude and his love of curiosity

J.W. and A.W.

Text copyright © 1996 by David A. Adler
Illustrations copyright © 1996 by John and Alexandra Wallner
ALL RIGHTS RESERVED
Printed in the United States of America

Library of Congress Cataloging-in-Publication Data
Adler, David A.
A picture book of Thomas Alva Edison/David A. Adler;
illustrated by John & Alexandra Wallner.
p. cm.
Summary: An introduction to the genius with a curious mind who
loved to experiment and who invented the phonograph, light bulb,
movie camera, and numerous other items.
ISBN 0-8234-1246-6 (hardcover: alk. paper)
1. Edison, Thomas A. (Thomas Alva), 1847–1931—Juvenile
literature. 2. Electric engineers—United States—Biography—
Juvenile literature. 3. Inventors—United States—Biography—
Juvenile literature. [1. Edison, Thomas A. (Thomas Alva),
1847–1931. 2. Inventors.] I. Wallner, John C., ill. II. Wallner,
Alexandra, ill. III. Title.
TK140.A627   1996   95-42533   CIP
621.3'092—dc20   AC
[B]
ISBN 0-8234-1414-0 (pbk.)

Thomas also experimented with fire inside his father's barn. The barn burned to the ground. His father was furious. He punished Thomas by giving him a thrashing in the town square.

Thomas was not a healthy child. He had many colds and when he was eight he had scarlet fever. He was deaf later, perhaps because of these early illnesses.

In 1854 the Edison family moved to Port Huron, Michigan. There seven-year-old Thomas went to school for the first time.

In class Thomas was restless. He didn't pay attention to the lessons. And he asked lots of questions. His teacher, Reverend Engle, had no patience for Thomas. He felt the boy was not smart enough to learn his lessons.

Thomas's mother told Reverend Engle that he didn't know how to teach a curious child. After three months, she took Thomas out of school and taught him herself.

Later Thomas went to two other schools. He once got into trouble for bringing a noisy chicken to class. But he did learn.

At home Thomas set up a laboratory in the cellar. Strange smells, smoke, and sometimes the sounds of small explosions came from there. Thomas was finding answers to some of his many questions.

Beginning in 1859, when Thomas was twelve, he worked as the candy butcher on the Grand Trunk Railroad. He sold candy, sandwiches, fruit, and newspapers to passengers.

Thomas set up a laboratory in the baggage car. He did experiments during the long stopover in Detroit. But Thomas didn't take proper care of the chemicals, and one day there was a fire. The baggage master quickly put it out. Then he threw the chemicals off the train.

In 1862 Thomas bought a secondhand printing press and some type. He set the press up in the baggage car and printed his own newspaper, the *Weekly Herald*. In it he printed news of people who traveled and worked on the train.

Thomas also wrote his opinions. He believed in work and wrote, "The more to do, the more done."

At each train stop, Thomas got off and sold newspapers to people near the station. With the money he earned, Thomas bought more chemicals for his experiments.

One morning, in 1862, at the Mount Clemens station, Thomas saw a boxcar rolling toward a small boy. Thomas dropped his things, ran, and saved the child. The boy's father rewarded Thomas by teaching him telegraphy. After that, beginning in 1863, Thomas worked for almost six years as a telegraph operator.

In 1869 Thomas moved to New York City. While he was there, he visited a company that sent out minute-by-minute information about changes in the price of gold. When the equipment in that office broke, Thomas quickly found the trouble and fixed it. He was given a high-paying job taking care of the company's equipment.

A few months later Thomas and a friend formed their own company. They made electrical devices for telegraphy. Thomas Edison worked from early morning until late at night. He invented a telegraph that printed the price of gold and silver.

Then Thomas went to work for himself. He invented an improved machine to send out minute-by-minute information on the price of stocks. He sold it to Western Union. With the money he set up a laboratory in Newark, New Jersey.

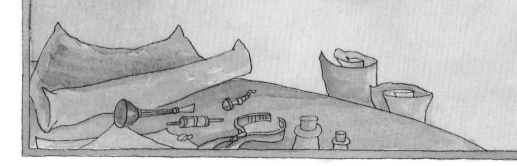

Thomas Edison worked on improving the telegraph. Among his inventions was an automatic telegraph system. It didn't need a telegrapher to take down the messages. He also invented the quadruplex, which could send four messages at the same time over one wire.

Edison's company sold printers to the Gold and Stock Company. In 1871 Thomas helped a friend's sister get a job there. She was a pretty sixteen-year-old named Mary Stilwell. Thomas kept stopping by Gold and Stock to check the printers and to see Mary Stilwell.

On December 25, 1871, Thomas and Mary married. They later had three children, Marion, Thomas, Jr., and William.

Thomas loved his wife, but his work always came first. Even on his wedding day he went to his shop to work on an experiment.

Thomas Edison had odd work habits. He started work late and often fell asleep on his laboratory bench. He ate around midnight.

In 1876 Thomas moved to Menlo Park, New Jersey, and set up a large, two-story laboratory. His work led to many inventions. He became known as "The Wizard of Menlo Park."

In 1876 Alexander Graham Bell invented the telephone. In 1877 Edison and his staff improved it. They invented the carbon transmitter. It sent a clearer sound and became part of the Bell telephone.

Then Thomas worked on a machine to save sounds and replay them. In 1877 he invented the phonograph.

In the 1870s homes were lit with candlelight and oil and gas lamps. But there were smoke, gas fumes, and the danger of fire. In 1878 Thomas Edison began searching for some way to use electricity to light homes.

Thomas Edison's notes filled hundreds of books. He said at the time, "I speak without exaggeration when I say that I have considered three thousand theories in connection with electric light."

He experimented for more than a year. "Genius," he said, "is one percent inspiration and ninety-nine percent perspiration."

The electric light bulb he invented in 1879 had baked cotton thread inside. When electricity passed through the bulb, the thread glowed.

People came to Menlo Park to see Edison's new invention. And when they saw the lights, they wanted them in their homes. Thomas Edison hired workers to make bulbs, lamps, wires, and other things needed for this new form of light.

In 1882 in New York City he set up the Pearl Street Station to generate electricity. In September electricity was used to provide light for the first eighty-five customers.

Edison's wife Mary had been ill for several years. Then, in July 1884, she contracted typhoid fever. She died on August 9, 1884. Following her death, Edison spent even more time with his work.

One evening the following year, while Thomas was visiting a friend in Boston, he met Mina Miller. She was a smart, well-educated woman. She was beautiful, too, with deep brown eyes and black hair. A few months later, while he was walking, he thought about Mina and was almost run over by a streetcar. Thomas Edison was in love.

Thomas married Mina on February 24, 1886. They moved to a large house in West Orange, New Jersey, and had three children together, Madeline, Charles, and Theodore.

Thomas developed a new phonograph with better sound. Then, in 1887, he placed a tiny phonograph inside a tin doll. With the turn of a crank, the doll seemed to talk.

Thomas Edison invented a movie camera and projector. In 1903 his company made the first movies to tell a story, *The Life of an American Fireman* and *The Great Train Robbery*.

He also invented the storage battery used in electric cars and submarines, a cement mixer, and a copying machine.

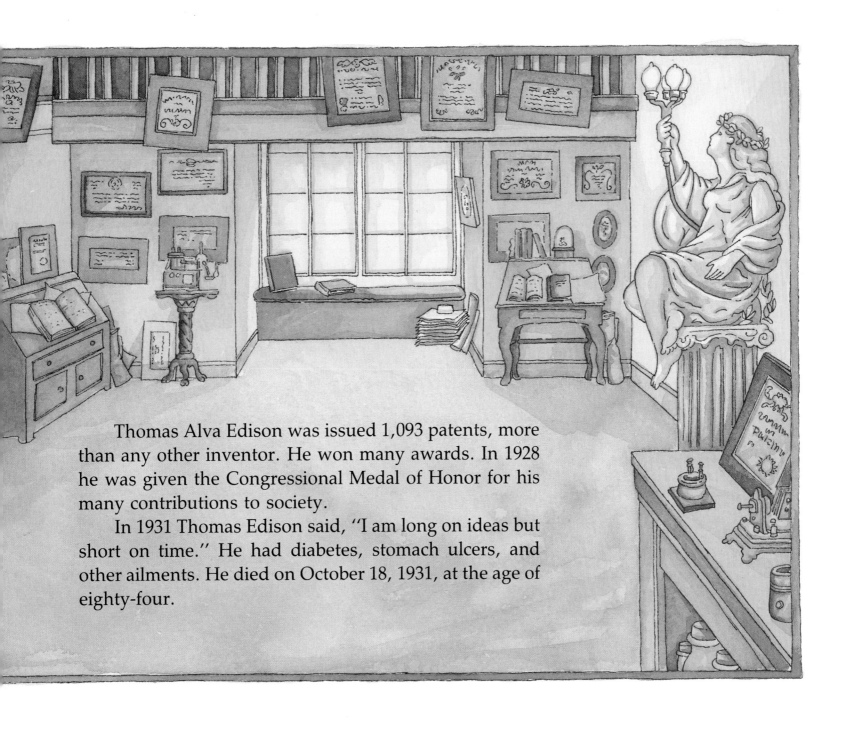

Thomas Alva Edison was issued 1,093 patents, more than any other inventor. He won many awards. In 1928 he was given the Congressional Medal of Honor for his many contributions to society.

In 1931 Thomas Edison said, "I am long on ideas but short on time." He had diabetes, stomach ulcers, and other ailments. He died on October 18, 1931, at the age of eighty-four.

To honor Thomas Edison, on the night of his funeral, lights all across the United States were turned off at ten o'clock.

Thomas Edison was an inventive genius. His inventions changed our world.

AUTHOR'S NOTE

Thomas was the youngest of seven children, but Thomas only knew three of his siblings, Marion, William, and Harriet. Carlisle and Samuel, Jr., died before he was born. And in 1847, the year Thomas was born, his sister Eliza died.

Edison nicknamed his eldest child "Dot" and his second child "Dash" after the signals used to send messages over the telegraph.

Lewis Miller, the father of Thomas Edison's second wife Mina, was also an inventor. He made improvements to the reaper to harvest grain with less waste.

IMPORTANT DATES

1847	Born in Milan, Ohio, on February 11.
1854	The Edisons move to Port Huron, Michigan.
1863–1868	Worked as a telegraph operator in Canada and the United States.
1871	Married Mary Stilwell on December 25.
1874	Invented the quadruplex.
1877	Invented the carbon telephone transmitter and the first phonograph.
1879	Invented the electric light bulb.
1884	Wife Mary died on August 9.
1886	Married Mina Miller on February 24.
1891	Invented a motion picture camera.
1928	Awarded the Congressional Medal of Honor.
1931	Died in West Orange, New Jersey, on October 18.